FOREWORD

When Jim first presented his Control Your Day method on the GTD® Virtual Study Group podcast in February 2009, I had no idea the impact his approach would have. Hundreds of people have requested the slide deck from that presentation and the episode remains one of the most popular we've ever done. I know that hundreds of Outlook users have already benefited tremendously from Jim's approach and I'm excited to see that he's gone on to write this eBook.

People come to me all the time trying to stay on top of handling all their email and, at the same time, manage their tasks. Control Your Day gives solid, practical guidance on how to do both--with less effort and with much greater effectiveness. Instead of worrying about moving back and forth between two (or more) tools, CYD allows you to manage everything from the place where you already spend so much time: your email inbox.

I've heard users rave about CYD for years and it's exciting to celebrate this new eBook launch. I've no doubt that Jim and his CYD method will impact so many people's lives and help them get their work done with greater ease.

Tara Rodden Robinson, Ph.D., ACC

Executive Productivity Coach and Host of the GTD® Virtual Study Group

Productivity HQ

Corvallis, Oregon

January 4, 2013

INTRODUCTION

Are you ready to Control Your Day?

◊ The Control Your Day(CYD)™ methodology uses built-in features of Microsoft Outlook to keep your email messages organized and help you focus on priorities. Ask yourself the following questions to see if, CYD is the right system for you.

◊ Do you spend a large amount of time moving messages from your inbox and sent folder to subject based folders?

◊ Does your inbox contain hundreds or thousands of messages that might need your attention?

Do you struggle with multiple points of focus between your inbox, task list and other tools you use to manage your daily priorities?

◊ Do you lose track of requests you have delegated?

◊ Does your email system stress you out?

If you answered yes to any of the questions above, this book will help you learn how to:

◊ Simplify filing your email.

◊ Manage incoming emails and tasks.

◊ Eliminate lost messages by using a series of virtual search folders in Outlook.

The key to the approach is grounded in the simplicity of implementation and use. If you can relieve yourself from using folders and begin to manage tasks directly from your email messages the advantages of CYD will offer positive results.

Benefits of the CYD System, you will:

◊ Manage all active emails/tasks from one view.

◊ Eliminate filing messages in subject folders.

◊ Get to Inbox Zero.

◊ Receive alerts when delegated tasks are not completed on schedule.

◊ Lower your Email Stress Level (ESL).

A bit about me

People know me as a productivity hacker. I started with simple index cards, moved to various paper systems and then to hardware/software systems to help organize and control my workload. Reading David Allen's book *Getting Things Done (GTD)* was a turning point for me. I became an instant GTDer and never looked back. If you have not read his books, I highly recommend ordering *Getting*

Things Done from Amazon TODAY! You will find many of David's concepts applied in my system including Inbox Zero, using one collection point, contexts, next actions and the weekly review.

Just to be clear I don't spend my days building systems, well at least not email productivity systems. I design supply chain systems for top retailers across North America. The CYD system is a part of my everyday life to stay organized. It works for me, it can work for you.

This E-Book includes everything you need to configure and run CYD. I setup a companion website with videos and printable step by step guides to support the book at www.controlyourday.net. Sign up as a CYD forum member and you can post any questions you have about CYD.

Outlook Versions Supported

The CYD methodology works in versions of Outlook from 2007 forward. It works in both standalone and Exchange installations. The step-by-step instructions in this book are based on Outlook 2010 screens, if you are using an older or newer version of Outlook the steps may vary slightly.

How to use this book

Read chapters 1 and 2 to get a basic understanding of the benefits of CYD and the steps it will take to implement your new email management system.

Before opening Microsoft Outlook and beginning implementation of CYD, read the rest of the book and review the step-by-step instructions. I want you to be able to visualize how your new email system will work before you begin the implementation.

At that point, open Microsoft Outlook and go through the step-by-step guidelines and setup CYD. The content is organized so that the changes will not affect how you use Outlook today. One of my early beta testers suggested that I make it possible to run CYD and still allow you to use Outlook as you have in the past so you can run a parallel test of CYD before fully implementing it. Once you are comfortable with the way CYD works, you can then make the switch.

Additionally, the last chapter offers email management tips and best practices for email and time management.

 If you are a corporate user of Outlook, check with your IT department before you make any changes to Outlook and implement CYD.

I would like to thank my wife, Suzanne, for all of her support and great feedback along the way and my two boys, who put up with me while I locked myself away nights and weekends to write this book.

Maggie, thank you for the edit and your suggestions to improve the chapter intros. As a long time CYD user, you provided constructive feedback that added focus and clarity to the concepts covered in this book. Thanks to Joan and Sharon for the proofreading efforts and to my beta users that implemented CYD directly from the book to make sure I didn't miss anything.

Tara, thank you for the wonderful Foreword and for all your help and support over the years through your GTD Virtual Study Group. (www.tararobinson.com)

Author and productivity guru Augusto Pinaud suggested to

restructure the step-by-step chapters with a basic and advanced section. The basic features will get you up and running with CYD. The advanced sections do require a bit more technical skills and possibly some assistance from your IT department if you are a corporate user to make a few configuration changes to Outlook and your Windows registry.

1

CYD - THE BIG PICTURE

Chapter Plan

◊   Explain the concepts of CYD

What is CYD and why do I need it?

The concept of CYD is a methodology to improve the use of Microsoft Outlook so that you keep attention on priorities, eliminate time wasted on random and not important messages and actually feel like you have control over your email.

You need it because you are overwhelmed by the number of emails sitting in your inbox, you are tired of carrying around the burden of trying to respond to them, and you are stressed about the possibility that you missed an important email.

Several years ago I faced my old inbox with frustration and fatigue. The feeling of never getting control of the numerous emails streaming in wore me out. Older mail kept getting pushed down further and further. I started to ignore older messages and would only focus on new messages, losing the ability to respond to important messages previously received. At the same time, I tried to create tasks to track commitments and work I had delegated. My workload management system became a two-window view, my task list and my inbox. This didn't work. The inbox always had my attention and my task list took a back seat. With the speed and volume of email, tasks quickly became outdated and so was this process.

Time for a change

As for many others, Outlook email is my primary tool to manage commitments and communications. In order to manage my tasks and action items, I send myself emails with the work or task listed in the subject field. I send these messages from any device I am using; laptop, mobile phone or Ipad. I found a great smart phone application called **eMemo** that allows you to send emails to yourself in just one step. Open the app, type a task into the subject (such as @ NA Book flight to Tacoma) and hit send.

I came up with the idea of the "Control Your Day" virtual search folder. This folder shows messages from my Inbox and Sent folder that require follow-up (my workload). It allows me to see all new and overdue messages (sent and received) in one folder. I set the folder to sort on due date instead of date received. This gave me control in reviewing the sequencing of messages and focused my attention in the right place. Outlook automatically color codes messages that are past due in red, a clear indicator for my attention. Thus CYD was born.

!CYD Virtual Search Folder

⏰	📄	🔗	Due D...	From	Subject	Next Action

Flag: Due Date: Today

	28-Dec...	Bike Nashbar	Save Up to 72% On What You Re...	@Web Chk for Shoes
	30-Dec...	TechSmith	Get started with Camtasia Studio i...	@Web Watch tutorial
	1-Jan-13	auto-confirm@a...	Your Order with Amazon.com	@Call Joe, package arri..
	1-Jan-13	Bike Nashbar	Get Ready for 2013 With An Extra...	
	1-Jan-13	Getting Things ...	[2] discussions and [7] comments...	@Read GTD article
	2-Jan-13	iStockphoto-Tra...	Welcome to iStock. Here's what y...	@NA load graphics
	2-Jan-13	vacycling@goo...	VAcycling: Abridged summary of ...	
	2-Jan-13	Amazon.com Re...	How many stars would you give ...	
	3-Jan-13	Getting Things ...	[4] discussions and [31] comment...	

Flag: Due Date: Tomorrow

	4-Jan-13	Gazelle	Here's $10 to help you with your ...
	4-Jan-13	Amazon.com	Your Amazon.com order of "TRE...

Flag: Due Date: This Week

New messages appear in the center of the view in bold (unread) and anything that has a due date in the future is pushed forward in the **CYD folder**. At times I have hundreds of messages that are due at a future date. I no longer stress out over those messages since they have already been pushed forward, and my attention is on overdue messages (red) and new emails arriving today.

The **CYD folder** worked great for me except when on the road or tied up in multi-day meetings. Just a few days away from my email and I would end up with hundreds of messages in the red and it would take me weeks to dig myself out. I recently added two additional folders to the system to help tread water during these times. This has been a great solution while traveling or unable to commit time required to keeping my email in order.

Introducing... The "Due Today" and "Today's Focus" folders

The virtual folders concept simplifies email management, especially while traveling or away from your computer. The **Due Today folder** contains Inbox and Sent messages that have a Due Date of today. An additional function is involved where this folder is sorted by date received and the Outlook Conversation Thread feature is turned on. The end result is a listing of all messages due today (just received or due date previously set to today). The Outlook conversation thread feature expands the current message and contains all other messages that are part of the same thread. If you wanted to send a response to the thread, you would respond to the latest message sent and ultimately create efficiency in your response. This also allows you to delete all previous messages in the same thread keeping only the last email containing the entire thread.

!Due Today Virtual Search Folder

The Today's Focus folder is a list of action items that require attention today, it shows messages with a follow-up flag that are due today and have the category !Today assigned. This folder works well if you like to plan your day before you dig into the workload. Look through your active folders and highlight messages you want to focus on and assign the !Today category to them.

You can use one, two or all three of these folders as you work through the day. Since they are virtual search folders in Outlook, if you clear out a message in one (by clearing the follow-up flag), it is removed from all three.

It would be great if you could process and complete each message immediately upon reading the email. Unfortunately for most of us, this is impossible. Next Actions and Contexts track action items you were not able to complete at the time of receiving the email. This way when you do come back to that message, you will see the action item without having to read the entire email again.

Tracking your "Next Action" in Outlook

While designing CYD, I needed a free form text field in Outlook that could easily be referenced and updated. I found a field called Contacts that is stored with each email message. Outlook uses this field to manually link an email message to a contact. I have never seen it used this way, and it works for my Next Actions methodology. The Contacts field is edited from the Message Options dialog box. It can be accessed from a number of views in Outlook. The step-by-step instructions are demonstrated in chapter 9.

Message Options Dialog Box

Now we have a place to store our Next Actions, we need to place Next Actions into contexts. David Allen talks extensively about Next Actions and contexts in his book *Getting Things Done*®, a book I highly recommend reading. The goal is to define a Next Action for each message that requires additional work and place it into a context or group for future action. The @NA context is a generic group that can be used to capture any next actions. It is up to you whether or not you want to break the contexts beyond the @NA context. Using the @ symbol and a brief prefix makes it very easy to setup a search folder that includes all messages associated to a context.

Action Context Examples
@Agenda Bill – discuss stats
@Call BellCo about invoice
@NA Submit expense report
@Read article on supply chain
@Web research leadership courses

One search folder can be created for each context defined. This ensures all messages with the same context to be visible in one folder. Chapter 6 explains how to setup your @Context folders.

Components of the CYD System

There are some aspects that may seem somewhat technical. My goal is to provide a high level understanding of how CYD works within Microsoft Outlook. If you are feeling a but confused or overwhelmed, keep reading. Once you understand the methodology of CYD and the value it will bring to your everyday life, implementation will make sense after you begin to work on it.

CYD uses three physical Outlook folders to store your messages. They are Inbox, InboxPro (Processed) and Sent. An active message is a message that has a due date and still requires work on your part. Once you complete that work, you clear the due date which then designates that message as completed in your CYD folders.

Outlook Folder	Purpose
Inbox	Active messages
InboxPro	Completed messages
Sent	All sent messages

In order to tag your emails by topic (a client, project name, family activity, etc.), CYD uses the Category function (not personal folders). Messages can be assigned one or more categories. This allows you to group and organize messages in your InboxPro and Sent folders under multiple topics, if necessary. The Outlook rules engine is a perfect way to auto-assign categories as messages are received. The rules engine can also aid in automatically moving completed messages from Inbox to InboxPro. A manual move of emails is an option and can be a part of your daily or weekly cleanup. The beauty of CYD and one of its major benefits to you is that all received emails are stored in your InboxPro folder and future searches are simple and easy.

CYD greatly simplifies message archiving. At the end of the calendar year, it is recommended to move the InboxPro and Sent folders to an archive PST file for easy storage. If you are an exchange user, you may need to archive those folders more often, especially if your IT shop limits the amount of space you can use on Exchange.

Use Outlook virtual search folders to build work spaces

Outlook Search Folders are virtual folders that can be created with preset criteria. Your messages are stored in the Inbox, InboxPro and Sent folders. The search folders are just a way to group messages by subject, project, or any other criteria. You have complete flexibility in viewing and working messages in Outlook. Personally, I make extensive use of the search folder feature in CYD. Each CYD folder searches your Inbox and Sent folder for any messages that have a due date assigned.

CYD Folder	Purpose
!CYD	Overdue, current and future active messages
!Due Today	Messages due today
!Today's Focus	Messages flagged by you for today's focus

The heart of CYD is based on the !CYD, !Due Today and !Today's Focus virtual search folders. Outlook uses a Due Date field to manage its follow-up flag feature and is used to prioritize messages across the CYD folders. Chapter 5 provides the step-by-step instructions to setup the CYD follow-up flag rule.

Here is a graphical representation of the CYD folder structure. Again, the Inbox and Sent folders are physical folders that hold all of your messages. The "! Folders" are virtual search folders that show active messages from Inbox and Sent.

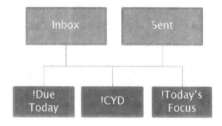

Are you convinced that CYD is for you? It is if you can relate to any of the following:

◊ I lose track of messages, especially if I do not address them immediately.

◊ My boss, peers or other contacts have to send multiple emails requesting the same thing.

◊ I have hundreds of unprocessed emails in my Inbox.

◊ I have too many action item lists and struggle to get anything accomplished on time.

◊ I can't keep track of work that I have delegated to others.

◊ I never have time to properly file my messages.

◊ I say to myself "I hate email"!

I truly believe that CYD can improve the way you manage email and your workload. If you are feeling a bit overwhelmed at this point, don't give up, keep reading. This book will walk you through every step of the process and explain the benefits and value along the way. Support videos are available on the CYD Forum at www. controlyourday.net.

Making CYD a part of life management

You are just 6 important steps away from implementing CYD. The steps are discussed in greater detail throughout the rest of the book.

◊ Setup Outlook categories to replace your existing folders.

◊ Create each of the virtual search folders you will need in CYD.

◊ Setup rules to flag inbound messages for follow-up and to auto-categorize messages

◊ Setup a process to move completed message to your InboxPro folder

◊ Move your existing Inbox to an archive folder (this is the scariest part)

◊ Start processing and managing your workload with CYD

The chapters ahead cover basic changes needed to implement CYD. At the end of each chapter, I cover features that are more advanced and may require access to administrative features of your computer. These are not required to implement CYD, however they will give you more control over how you setup and configure the CYD system.

2

TWELVE STEPS TO CYD

Chapter Plan

◊   Understand the action plan

Controlling your day is no longer a dream, it is a reality. Yes, you can know everything that is in your Outlook Inbox with CYD. Your commitment to the following steps is all that is needed. Of course it takes time to adjust and release old habits. In fact, my colleagues who use CYD claim that the time invested in switching to CYD has paid off tenfold. The weight of daunting emails waiting for you can be lifted. It is up to you. You can download a printable version of the checklist from www.controlyourday.net.

1. Create a folder named InboxPro under your Inbox.

2. Create a rule to flag each message you receive for follow-up today.

3. Create the auto-filing macro (optional advanced feature).

4. Add Due Date and Contact fields to your default compact view.

5. Add the Message Options icon to your toolbar.

6. Create the !CYD Folder include messages from Inbox and Sent that have a follow-up flag.

7. Create the !Due Today folder (same as !CYD) and then sort by date and show conversations.

8. Create the !Today folder, (same as !CYD) and add category = !Today.

9. Create your @Context folders filtering active messages by context.

10. Remove follow-up flags from existing inbox/sent messages that no longer require action.

11. Create an archive folder and move all your existing inbox messages to this folder.

12. Start using CYD !

3

MOVING FROM FOLDERS TO CATEGORIES

Chapter Plan

◊   Present the benefits and limitations of using categories

Have you found yourself asking "now which personal folder did I put that email in" and then how long did it take to find that email. Using categories is the preferred replacement and they are a great time saver when you need to retrieve old email. Honestly, if this is the only CYD concept that you implement, the value would keep you smiling for a long time. Of course, the complete CYD system will gain substantially more value in managing your email and your life.

If you have rules setup today to automatically file messages that do not need to be actioned (newsletters, group distribution emails, etc.). You can leave those rules in place. Be sure those messages are filed and not set with a follow-up flag. This way they will not appear in your CYD folders.

Constraints when using folders to store and organize messages

◊   A message can only be stored in one folder, but it could relate to more than one folder.

◊   You have to maintain your folder structure.

◊   Archiving messages can be difficult if you have many different folders, it can be hard to decide where to put messages.

◊   You can't view all your messages in one folder.

Here are a few of the benefits of using categories

◊   You can assign multiple categories to the same message.

◊   You can create temporary category names for things like projects or trips and then remove them.

◊   You can auto-assign categories as messages are received based on sender, subject and other criteria.

◊   You can store all your messages in just two folders (InboxPro and Sent) and then use categories to group your messages.

There is one negative to using categories, you can't nest categories like you can folders. For example you could create a folder called Customers and then create sub-folders under Customers for each customer. My solution for this is to add a single letter prefix to each category name. Then when you sort by category in your folders, you will see you category names in order by the first letter code.

For example, I create one category name for each of my customer Accounts and prefix those names with "a." Here is a list of a few examples, feel free to use any prefix that makes sense to you. You can use the first letter of you company name for work related categories that don't fit a specific group and even use one of your initials for personal categories.

Prefix	Group
a.	Account / Customers
p.	Projects
s.	Staff
v.	Vendors

And here is what that looks like in my Category view in Outlook.

Color Categories

To assign Color Categories to the currently selected
category. To edit a category, select the category na

	Name
☐	@Call
☐	@NA
☐	@Read
☐	@Someday-Maybe
☐	a.Becker&Son
☐	a.Sunshine Imports
☐	p.AsiaTrip
☐	p.Budgets
☐	p.CYDMarketing
☐	s.Reviews
☐	v.BoxesRUs
☐	v.PC Services

The Outlook rules engine can be used to automatically assign one or
multiple categories as messages are received. For example you could
create a rule that assigns the category a.Becker&Son if the sender
email address includes "beckerson.com". Check the step-by-Step
section in chapter 5 for instructions on how to create a rule to auto-
assign a category.

If you already use categories, it's OK to leave those category names out there, but overtime you should clean out that list and align the category names to the formats listed above. This is a good time to setup a few categories that you will use to manage next actions and prioritize work for today.

Adding new categories

It is very simple to add, rename and delete categories in Outlook. Just a couple of quick notes first. If you rename a category, that new name will be applied to every message associated to that category. If you delete an existing category from your master list, that category description will not be removed from existing messages. This is a good feature, it allows you to remove categories from your master list that you no longer need, but this will not affect messages you have already categorized and filed.

Add the main CYD Categories to your list

1. Open up your category list through one of the following methods.

    ◊   Right click on a message, select *Categories* and then select *All Categories.*

    ◊   Click the Home tab, click the *Categorize Icon* and then select *All Categories.*

2. The Categories window shows a listing of all of your categories, you can add, rename or delete categories from this view

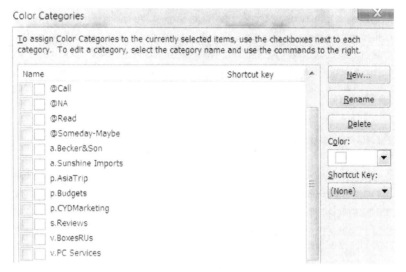

3. Click the **New** button and then type in the category name **@call.**

4. Click the **color drop down** and set it to **none** (using color takes up more space and adds noise to your CYD folders).

5. Click **OK** to save the new category name.

6. Complete steps 3 - 5 to add the following category names @NA, @Read, @Web, @Someday-Maybe, !Today.

7. Once you have finished adding categories, click **OK** to close the Category dialog window.

Your categories are now setup for CYD, as noted above, you can always go back and add, change and delete categories as needed.

4

CONFIGURE OUTLOOK FOR CYD

Chapter Plan

◊   Get CYD setup in your Microsoft Outlook

This is where the fun begins. It is time to setup Outlook for CYD. It is important to know that the steps we will complete in this chapter will not affect the way you currently work in Outlook. This will allow you to setup and use CYD but still give you the ability to work directly from your Inbox while you kick the tires of CYD.

If you are a visual person and prefer to see the steps below live, then go to www.controlyourday.net and sign up as a CYD member, you will then be granted access to view web videos that take you through the steps listed below and in the subsequence chapters.

Add CYD fields to your default view

Microsoft Outlook uses preset views to browse through email messages. Most users are setup with the "compact" view as their default view. The instructions below are based on that default configuration.

We are going to add the Due Date and Contacts field to your default view and rename the Contacts field to "Next Action". Then we will move the Categories field next to the Next Action field. We will then save and apply that view to your mailbox so that whenever you create a search folder, those fields are visible and in the right sequence.

1. Click the **View** menu option from above the Outlook ribbon, select **Change View**, select **Manage Views** from the options list.

2. Click the **Compact View** name, click **Modify.**

3. Click the **Columns Button**, find and highlight the **Due Date** field from the window on the left and then click the **Add button** to move **Due Date** from the Available Columns to the Show these columns list.

4. Drag the **Due Date** column and place it just above the From column.

5. Click the **Columns Button**, find and highlight the **Contacts** field from the window on the left and then click the **Add button** to move **Contacts** from the Available Columns to the Show these columns list.

6. Drag the **Contacts** column and place it just below **Subject.**

7. Drag the **Categories** column and place it below the **Contacts** column and click **OK**.

8. Click the **Format Columns** button and then click on the **Contact** column in the available fields list. Change the label from **Contacts** to **Next Action**, Click **OK** on all three windows to close out the Manage All Views window.

9. Click the **Change View** option again, and select **Apply current view to other mail folders**.

10. The top folder (your mailbox) should be checked, click **OK** to apply the new view to your mailbox.

11. Any new folder you create from this point forward will have the Due Date, Next Action and Categories columns displayed correctly.

Create your !CYD Folder

1. Right click on the **Search Folder**s link in the folder tree and select **New Search Folder**.

2. Drag the scroll bar to the bottom of the New Search Folder Options and select **Create a custom Search Folder** and then click the **Choose button** at the bottom of the window.

3. Enter **!CYD** as the Name of the search folder.

4. Click the **Criteria Button** and then click the **More Choices** Tab, check the box "**Only Items Which: are flagged by me** and then click **OK**.

5. Click the **Browse button**, check the box next to **Inbox** and **Sent Items**, make sure to uncheck the box at the very top, the default is to search all folders. Leave the **include Subfolders** box checked. Click **OK** and then **OK** again to save your changes.

6. Click the **!CYD** folder to show its contents in the main screen,

if you have any messages in the folder, they are messages that are in your sent or inbox that you may have flagged in the past. You can leave them for now, you will clean out these flags before you start using CYD.

Create the !Due Today Folder

1. Right click on the **Search Folders** link in the folder tree on the left side of outlook and select **New Search Folder.**

2. Drag the scroll bar to the bottom of the New Search Folder Options and select **Create a custom Search Folder** and then click the **Choose button** at the bottom of the window.

3. Enter **!Due Today** as the Name of the search folder.

4. Click the **Criteria Button** and then click the **More Choices** Tab, check the box **Only Items Which: are flagged by me.**

5. Click the **Advanced Tab** in the Search Folder Criteria window and the click the **Field button**, select **All Mail Fields,** click the **Due Date** Field, set the condition = "Today", click the **Add to List button** and finally click **OK.**

6. Click the **Browse button**, check the box next to **Inbox** and **Sent Items,** make sure to uncheck the box at the very top as this defaults to search all folders. Leave the **include Subfolders** box checked. Click **OK** and then OK again to save your changes.

7. Click the **!Due Today** folder, click the **View menu,** click **Date** from the Arrangement Box. Check the box to turn on **Show in Conversations.**

8. Right click on the **Due Date** column header and click **Remove this column**, all messages in this folder are due today.

9. Click the **View tab** in the Ribbon, click **View Settings**, click the **Group By button** and uncheck the box **Automatically Group According to Arrangement**.

 Sort order must be set to Date, if you change the sort, the conversation thread feature is disabled. To reset, click the View Tab and select Date from the Arrangement Box

Create the !Today Focus Folder

1. Right click on the **Search Folders** link in the folder tree and select **New Search Folder**.

2. Drag the scroll bar to the bottom of the New Search Folder Options and select **Create a custom Search Folder,** click the **Choose button** at the bottom of the window.

3. Enter **!Today Focus** as the Name of the search folder.

4. Click the **Criteria Button,** click the **More Choices Tab**, check the box **Only Items Which: are flagged by me.**

5. Click the **Categories button** in the same window, Click **New** to add a new category and add the category **!Today**, change the color to green or any other color you like. This is the one category I like to assign a color to so it stands out in all folder views.

6. Find the **!Today category** in your list and check the box next to it, click **OK**.

7. Click the **Advanced Tab** in the Search Folder Criteria window, click the **Field button**, select **All Mail Fields** and then click the **Due Date** Field, set the **condition =** **"Today"**, click the **Add to List button,** click **OK.**

8. Click the **Browse button**, check the box next to **Inbox** and **Sent Items,** make sure to uncheck the box at the very top as this defaults to search all folders. Leave the **include Subfolders** box checked. Click **OK** and then **OK** again to save your changes.

Create the InboxPro Folder

This will be your new storage folder for all received messages that you have marked as completed.

1. Click the **Inbox** from the Outlook folder tree on the left side of the screen.

2. Right click on the Inbox and select **New Folder.**

3. Enter the name as **InboxPro** and make sure **Inbox** is highlighted under **Select where to place folder** so this folder gets created below the Inbox.

4. Please double check the spelling of the folder name as it has to match exactly for the auto-filing macro to work properly (Chapter 5).

Questions

◊ *Why limit the folder search to just the Inbox and Sent folders?*

One of the benefits of CYD is that all of your messages are stored in just those two folders. If you have other folders that you created in the past that have messages with follow-up flags, they would then become visible in the CYD folders, this is ok, but could create confusion in the long run.

◊ *Why include subfolders in the folder browse if we are only going to reference messages in the Inbox and Sent folders?*

At the end of the year, you will move all your inboxPro and sent messages to separate storage folders (InboxPro-YY & Sent-YY). Chances are you will still have messages from the previous year that will pass over to the next year. As long as you leave these folders under the inbox and sent box, they will be visible to all of your CYD folders. Chapter 12 covers end of year cleanup in detail.

◊ *Which Folder should I work from first?*

This will be explained in detail in chapter 9. Ideally you would allocate a number of points in the day when you would work through your !Due Today folder to prioritize and work messages that are due today. After that you can choose to work from the !CYD folder, the !Today's Focus folder or any of your @context folders. This will all be explained shortly. Just remember these are all just different views of your messages, so if you clear a message from one CYD folder it is cleared from all of them.

◊   *Why use the Contacts field to track Next Actions?*

Great question, I needed a free form editable text field available to the user in the default configuration of Outlook. I didn't want to go through the steps of creating a user defined field as that would add additional complexity to the the process. The Contacts field is easily edited from the Message Options window which can be accessed when viewing messages in any of the folders or when you are editing a message. It is possible someone may be using that field for other purposes, but I haven't come across the field being used in my experience.

The toughest part of the setup is behind you. You now have the foundation built to support your new CYD system. In the next chapter we will setup the CYD Follow-up Today Rule and discuss the options available to file completed messages.

5

SETUP CYD RULE AND FILING MACRO

Chapter Plan

◊   Setup Outlook rules to support CYD

The Outlook rules engine allows you to create rules that can be fired when messages are received or sent. You can automatically set follow-up flags, assign categories, move messages and save attachments just to name a few.

We will start with the most important rule for CYD. This rule will be applied to all incoming messages; it will set a follow-up flag on each message and set the due date to the current date. The 3 main CYD folders only include messages from the Inbox and Sent Box that have a due date. The messages in these folders are sorted by that same due date.

Outlook Rules

The Outlook rules engine allows you to setup a rule that can be applied to incoming messages based on the criteria you set. The CYD Follow-up Rule, by default, will be applied to all messages as they arrive. It will set a follow-up flag due date for Today. The CYD search folders include all messages that have a Due Date. You can add exceptions to this rule to exclude certain types of messages if you want. For example, you might want to add an exception to exclude messages received from a particular user or with a certain subject if you do not want those messages included in your CYD folders.

The rules engine will fire all rules that apply to each message. If you want to exclude a message from the CYD Follow-up flag, you can add an exception to the rule below to skip those messages.

Create the CYD Follow Up Today Rule

1. Click the **Home tab** and then click the **Rules icon** and select **Create Rule**.

2. Click the **Advanced Options button** from the Create Rule window.

3. Click the **Next button** to skip the first window in the Rules Wizard and then click **Yes** to confirm this rule will apply to every message you receive.

4. Check the box **Flag message for follow up at this time**.

5. Click the hyperlink **follow up at this time** in the Step 2 box at the bottom and click **OK** to set **Today** as the for: value.

6. Click the **Next button**, if you want to apply any exceptions you can add them here

7. For example, if you want to exclude messages sent to a distribution list, check the box for **except if sent to people or public group** and then click the link in Step 2 to select the people or group to exclude.

8. Click the **Next button** to move to the final Rules screen.

9. Rename the rule to **CYD Follow Up Today**.

10. Make sure the first check-box **run this rule now** is unchecked and the second check-box **Turn on this rule** is checked. You don't want the rule to run until you clean out your existing Inbox messages.

11. Click the **Finish Button** to save the rule.

Setup rules to auto-assign categories

1. Right click on a message in your inbox, select **Rules** and then **Create Rule**.

2. The first dialog box allows you to set the rule based on the sender, recipient, subject. You can select one of these options or click the **Advanced Options button** to get more options.

3. For this example, check off the From "person's name" box and then click the **Advanced Options button**. You can click the **Next button** to skip the Set Condition dialog box since you already selected the sender name in the step above.

4. Check the box **assign it to a <u>category</u>**, then click the <u>**category**</u> link in the step 2 window at the bottom.

5. Check off the category you want to use or click the **New button** and add a new category and then check it off. You can check off more than one category.

6. Click the **Next Button**, click **Next** again to skip the Exceptions dialog window.

You can leave the default name of the rule or change it. If you want the rule to process against all existing messages in your inbox, you can check off that box.

Click the **Finish button** to save the rule.

You can repeat this process to build as many auto-categorize rules as you want. You don't have to categorize every message you receive. They will all be stored and accessible through your Inbox and Sent folders, the categories just provide for a better level of grouping.

Filing your Completed Messages

The InboxPro folder created in Chapter 4 will be used to store messages once they are completed. A message is completed when you have cleared the follow-up flag. The main reason for moving completed messages from your Inbox is to limit the messages you see on your smart phone (if connected to Outlook) to only those messages that still require follow-up. If you really wanted to, you could just leave the messages in your Inbox and at the end of the year move all messages with no follow-up flag to your archive folder. I think it's cleaner to file them daily or weekly and maintain just active messages in your Inbox. So why did I just go through all of that? In order to setup the auto-filing Macro, you will need administrator rights to Outlook, if you are a corporate user, your IT department may have to get involved. If you have the rights to make the changes, it is still a bit technical. If you want to give it a shot just follow the steps in the Auto-Filer Macro section. The alternative is to move the messages manually at the end of the day or the end of the week by following the steps listed below.

Manual Filing Process

1. Click on your **Inbox**.

2. Click on the **Flag icon** in the column heading section. This will sort your inbox message by follow-up flag status.

3. You should see some messages with an empty flag and others with a red flag. If you don't see the empty flag on any messages, click the **flag icon** again, to reverse the sort.

4. Highlight all of the messages with an empty flag, right click and select **Move** and select the **InboxPro** folder.

5. That's it, you have just filed all of your completed messages, could it BE any easier?

If you would like to automate the filing process, you can follow the steps below. This gets a bit tricky, and you may run into some issues if your IT department has locked down your ability to access admin features within Outlook.

This macro will run automatically once it is setup. DO NOT proceed with these steps until you are ready to implement CYD. This macro will move all completed messages from your Inbox to your InboxPro folder when you exit Outlook.

Create CYD Auto-Filing Macro

1. Your will first need to allow macros to run in Outlook, if you do not have admin access to your machine and Outlook you may need to get assistance from your IT department.

2. Click the **File Tab**, then select **Options**, then **Trust Center**.

3. Click the **Trust Center Options button.**

4. Click **Macro Settings** and then select the radio button option **Notifications for all Macros** .

5. This will allow the macro to run when you start outlook but will first give you a warning and ask you to confirm before starting Outlook each time.

6. Click **OK** on each window to close the options window.

7. Turn on the Developer Tab

    ◊   Click the **File tab**, then select **Options, Customize Ribbon.**

    ◊   On the right side of the screen you will see the main tabs, check the box next to the **Developer Tab**, then click **OK** to close the Options window.

8. Click the **Developer Tab** and then click the **Visual Basic icon.**

9. From the folder view on the left side, click the **Project1 folder**, then the **Microsoft Outlook Objects folder** and

6

SETUP @CONTEXT FOLDERS

Chapter Plan

◊   Setup @Context folders

The CYD Context folders can be used to group your messages in a way that will allow for easier processing. See chapter 9 for additional information on how to use the context folders in your daily work processes.

Suggested Context folders

Search Folder	Purpose
@Agenda	Topics to be discussed with others
@Calls	Telephone calls you need to make
@NA	Any message with a Next Action
@Web	Action requires access to the web
@Read	Articles/content you need to read
@WF	Messages waiting for a response
@Someday-Maybe	A folder to store wish list items

Create Your Next Actions Search Folder

This search folder will include all active messages from your Inbox and Sent Items folder with any value in the Contacts(Next Action) field.

1. Right click on **Search Folders** in the Outlook folder tree on the left side of the screen and click **New Search Folder.**

2. Scroll to the bottom of the screen and double click **Create a custom Search Folder** under the Custom option.

3. Enter the folder name, for example **@NA** *Include only active messages*

4. Click the **Criteria button,** click on the **More Choices Tab.**

5. Check off **Only items which: are flagged by me.** *|Include all messages that have a value in the Contacts field (Next Action)*

6. Click the **Advanced Tab,** click the **Field** button to open the fields dropdown.

7. Select **All Mail fields** and then select **Contacts** and set the condition to **is not empty,** click the button **add to List,** click the **OK** Button.

8. Click the **Add to List** button

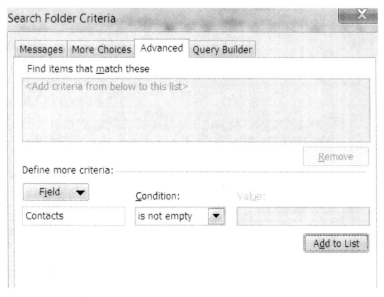

9. Click the **OK** button to return to the Custom Search Folder window.

10. Click the **Browse** button to select the physical folders to include, un-check your mailbox and then check the **Inbox** and **Sent Items**. Make sure to leave the **Search subfolders** box checked.

11. Click the **OK** button to close the Select Folders window, Click **OK** to close the Custom search folder window.

Create Specific Context Folders

Follow the steps below to create each Context folder

1. Right click on **Search Folders** in the Outlook folder tree on the left side of the screen and click **New Search Folder.**

2. Scroll to the bottom of the screen and double click **Create**

a custom Search Folder under the Custom option.

3. Enter the folder name, **@Agenda** *Include only active messages*

4. Click the **Criteria button**, click on the **More Choices Tab**.

5. Check off **Only items which: are flagged by me.** |*Include messages that match the criteria for the search folder*

6. Click the **Advanced Tab,** click the **Field** button to open the fields dropdown.

7. Select **All Mail fields** and then select **Contacts** and leave the condition as **contains** and then type **@Agenda** in the **Value** box.

8. Click the **Add to List** button.

9. Click the **OK** button to return to the Custom Search Folder window.

10. Click the **Browse** button to select the physical folders to include, un-check your mailbox and then check the **Inbox** and **Sent Items**. Make sure to leave the **Search subfolders** box checked.

11. Click the **OK** button to close the Select Folders window, Click **OK** to close the Custom search folder window.

Repeat the steps above for each @Context folder, you can build all of the search folders listed above or just select the contexts you want to focus on. Change the folder name in Step 3 and the criteria in Step 7 to match the context folder you are creating.

Follow the same steps to create the Someday-Maybe folder, skip steps 4 and 5. This will allow you to clear the follow-up flag on Someday-Maybe messages. They will appear in the Someday-Maybe context folder but they will not appear in your CYD, Due Today or !Today's Focus folders. If you want to remove an item from your Someday-Maybe folder, you can either delete it or remove the Someday-Maybe category assignment.

Advanced Section

The context folders created above search only in the Contacts(Next Action) field. You can expand their capabilities by adding multiple search criteria to each folder. This is most helpful if you are emailing tasks to yourself from places other than Outlook (your smart phone, webmail, etc.). The advanced version of the context folder will search the contacts field or the subject of the message for @context values.

Microsoft Outlook provides an advanced query builder but it is disabled by default. To enable this feature, you will need to make a change to your Windows Registry. If you are not familiar with editing the Registry please skip this section and work with the context folders as they are described above.

The instructions I provide below for the registry are advanced, if you are not familiar with the commands, do not attempt to make these changes.

Turn on Query Builder in Microsoft Windows

1. Close Outlook.

2. Start the Windows Registry editor.

3. Locate the registry subkey: (14.0 = Office 2010) HKEY_ CURRENT_USER4.0.

4. Right click on Outlook and choose New Key and enter QueryBuilder.

5. Close the registry editor and restart Outlook.

Expand the critera for your @Calls Context Search Folder

1. Right click on your **@Calls** Search Folder and choose **customize this search folder**.

2. Click the **Criteria** button, you should now see a Query Builder Tab.

3. Click the Advanced Tab and Remove the existing criteria, **Contacts contains @Call.**

4. Click the **Query Builder tab**.

5. Click **Field** button, select **All Mail Fields**, Select **Contacts**, criteria **Contains @Call,** Click **Add to List** Button.

6. Repeat step 5 for the Subject field, same criteria.

7. Change the **Logical Group** to **OR,** Click OK and OK again to save the folder changes.The @Calls folder will now show any active messages that have @Call in the Subject or the Contact field.

You can repeat this process for any of the other folders to add multiple search values.

7

SETUP PROJECT FOLDERS

Goals for this chapter

◊   Build and use project folders

Project folders can be used to group messages together for any purpose. Use them to collect messages for upcoming meetings, trips, customer visits, active projects and work you have assigned to others. Since they are virtual search folders, you can build them and tear them down as needed.

I have two sets of criteria for my project folders. The first is to include only messages that are flagged for follow-up. This way the messages only appear in that folder while they are active. Once I complete the message from any of my CYD folders, it is removed from the project folder. The second format is to include all messages with or without a follow-up flag. I often use this format when collecting messages for an upcoming trip or meeting. I don't need those messages coming back up as a reminder in my CYD folder, I just need them grouped together so that when I am preparing for the trip or meeting, I can quickly reference them. Here is an example of how the project folders appear in Outlook.

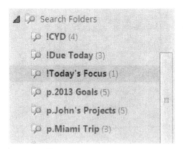

Create a Project Folder

1. Right click on **Search Folders** in the Outlook folder tree on the left side of the screen and click **New Search Folder.**

2. Scroll to the bottom of the screen and double click **Create a custom Search Folder** under the Custom option.

3. Enter the folder name, for example **p.2013 Budget Plans**.

4. Click the **Criteria button**, click on the **More Choices Tab**.

5. If you want to include messages with a follow-up flag, check off **Only items which: are flagged by me**, if you want to include all messages from your Inbox, InboxPro and Sent folders, leave this box unchecked.

6. Set any additional criteria for this folder. In most cases you will probably click the categories button and create a new category to assign to messages that will be included in this folder. You can you any of the folder criteria options available.

7. Your screen should look similar to the figure above. Click **OK** to close out the criteria screen.

8. Click the **Browse button** to set the physical folder to include in the search.

9. Remove the check next to your mailbox and check off the **Inbox** and the **Sent Items** folder. Make sure the **Search Subfolders box** is checked at the bottom of the screen. See figure below.

10. Click **OK** on each of the screens to save your new project folder

You can follow the steps above to create project folders whenever you want to group messages together. To remove a project folder, just right click on it and select Delete Folder. Be careful never to choose Delete All from this menu unless you want to delete the messages along with the folder.

8

CLEAN UP YOUR INBOX/SENT FOLDER

Chapter Plan

◊   Clean up your current Outlook system

Depending on how many messages you have in your inbox, this could be quick or it could take some time to prep for the transition. First here is the plan: you will create an Inbox-Old below your inbox and move all your existing inbox messages to that folder. Next we need to make sure there are no follow-up flags already set on any messages in your sent folder as they will start to appear in your CYD folders. Once that is done, you can start processing all new mail and all of your commitments through CYD.

If you have already been using follow-up flags to keep track of messages that require additional work, you need to decide if you want those messages to flow into your new CYD folders. Since we created the Inbox-Old as a subfolder of the Inbox, it will be included in the CYD folders. If you don't want to see those messages in your new system, just clear the follow-up flags from your Inbox-Old and Sent folders as described below.

Clean out your existing Inbox

1. Create Inbox-Old

    ◊   Right click on your **inbox** and select **New Folder.**

    ◊   Enter **Inbox-Old** as the name and make sure **Inbox** is highlighted to create the new folder under your **Inbox** folder.

2. Click on your **Inbox** to show all your messages.

3. Select all the messages, you can click on the first message once, then click the scroll bar to the right and drag the window down to the last message. Hold down the **Shift key** and click your mouse on the last message to highlight them all.

 This next step could take some time if you have a larger number of email messages stored in your Inbox

4. Right click on a selected message and then select **Move** and pick **Inbox-Old** from the dropdown list. When you select the folder, Outlook will start moving your messages.

5. Once Outlook finishes, you will have a completely empty

Inbox.

6. If any of the messages from your Inbox had a follow-up flag set, they will still appear in your CYD folders. If you don't want them to show up, you need to clear the follow-up flag on all messages stored in your Inbox-Old folder. You can follow the steps listed below for the Sent folder.

Your Inbox is EMPTY, take a moment and enjoy this feeling it doesn't happen very often.

Remove Follow-up Flags from any Sent messages

1. Click on your **Sent folder.**

2. Highlight all messages in your Sent folder (see steps above).

3. Right click on a highlighted message, click **Follow-up** and then select **Clear Flag**.

4. This will remove any follow-up flags you may have set in the past out outbound messages. You could leave these follow-up flags in place if you want the messages included in your CYD folders.

You are now ready to start using CYD. The next chapter teaches you how to use the system you have just setup.

9

CONTROL YOUR DAY

Chapter Plan

◊   Manage your daily work processes

This is the operating section of CYD. First a high level overview of how to operate the system and then I will break down each component and hopefully answer any questions that you may have. CYD focuses on managing your daily work flow, while it will help you to drive projects and commitments forward; it is not designed to be a high level project management tool.

When you are ready to start testing CYD, please remember you can run it along side your current system. As long as you clear the follow-up flag when you are done with a message, the CYD folders will show you just your active messages. You can work from your Inbox as you do today or work from your CYD folders. Continue to file messages as you have in the past as you go through the dry run. When you make the decision to move over to CYD then you can switch from your current filing folder structure to using the InboxPro folder.

My original goals for CYD

◊   Manage all of my commitments and delegated workload from one view.

◊   Reduce the amount of time spent "working" my inbox and organizing or filing the content.

◊   Deliver a higher level of service to my customers, peers, directs and my boss.

Here is a synopsis of my day using CYD

I start my day by first checking my calendar to determine open and blocked time slots not a direct part of CYD but still an important step in my daily process. Next I open the !Due Today folder. This folder shows me messages due today that I had received or sent previously or that have arrived today. I will work those messages (explained below). Once that is completed, I will then move to my !Today's Focus folder to work on or review tasks I had prioritized for today. From there I will work from either my context folders or my !CYD folder to work through my backlog.

I try to check my Due Today folder at least three times a day to stay on top of new email, you will have to make the decision yourself as to how often you need to check in on new messages. At the end of the day. I review my !CYD folder and focus in on the backlog (anything in red) and usually select a few items to flag as Today's Focus so they are include in that folder for the next day.

First we need to make sure you have done the critical steps in the earlier chapters, if you have not completed the following, please go back to the earlier chapters and complete these steps first.

◊ Modified the default view to include the Due Today and Next Action fields in your CYD folder views.

◊ Created the !CYD and !Due Today search folders.

◊ Created the outlook rule to flag all messages for follow-up when they are received. If you have completed that step and you've done a send/receive, you should now have messages visible in your CYD Folders (!CYD, !Due Today).

Processing work that has come due today

1. Open your !Due Today folder. This folder shows all messages sent and received that have a due date of today, this includes messages you have received in the past and flagged with a future due date and messages received today. This folder is sorted by received date and set to show full message threads, so you will see all related messages below the current message.

2. When you open up a message thread, you can delete or clear the follow-up flag on any earlier messages and just work from the current message. If there are attachments on earlier messages, you may want to move them to the latest message or file them in a Windows folder before deleting the earlier messages. Alternately you could just clear the follow-up flag on those messages which would leave them in your inbox for filing to InboxPro.

The first line of the conversation thread is s summary line. If you delete this line, you will delete all messages in that thread. Click the small arrow to the left to open the thread to review the messages that will be deleted.

3. Work through your messages and apply the Four D's.

Action	Outcome
Do It	2 minutes or less, just do it!
Delegate It	Forward and set follow-up flag
Defer It	Set Next Action and follow-up flag
Delete It	Clear flag to file it or just delete it

4. Work through as much of your Due Today folder as you can in the time you have allocated. Ideally you want to clear out this folder each day, but sometimes that will be impossible. When this does happen, those overdue items will be visible in your !CYD Folder for processing when you have the time.

Tracking Messages you Send

When you send an email you can add a follow-up flag for a future date. The message will then appear in your CYD folder and when it comes due, it will provide a reminder to you . You can take this one step further and add a context @WF and a brief note, this way when the message comes due you can easily see what you requested.

1. Create your message.

2. Click the **Follow-up** drop down from the **Tag** section

of the ribbon and select your follow-up date (tomorrow, next week, custom, etc.).

3. If you want to add a Next Action, click the **Message Options arrow** in the bottom right of the **Tag** section of the ribbon, enter @WF and a brief note.

4. Adding the Waiting For (WF) context to the message will help to refresh your memory when this message bubbles back up in your CYD folder.

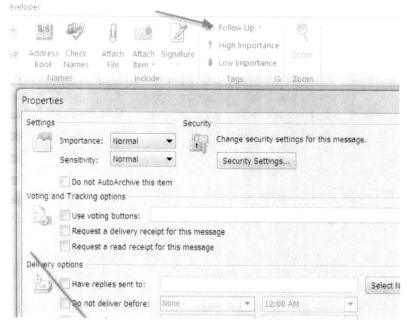

If and hopefully when your recipient responds to your message, their message will appear in your !CYD and !Due Today folders. If you process it from your Due Today folder, you will see the entire conversation thread, you should delete the message you sent or clear the follow-up flag to remove the reminder from your message. If you are working from your CYD folder, you can click on the subject to quickly sort by subject and then delete or clear the flag for the original message you sent.

Working your @Context Folders

The context folders are designed to allow you to group work tasks together that can be done collectively. For example you may want to set a time of day where you make phone calls, you would open up your @Calls folder and work through the messages in that folder during this work period, another concept originated by David Allen.

The filter on most @Context folders includes messages that have a follow-up flag checked and have text in the contacts field that matches the pre-set criteria. The one exception to this is the Someday-Maybe folder. That folder includes all messages that have the @Someday-Maybe category checked off. We exclude the follow-up flag requirement on this message, that way once you flag an item as Someday-Maybe, you can remove the follow-up flag and avoid having to be reminded of it week after week.

Here are a Few Examples

@Agenda

1. A message arrives that requires a discussion with another team member, but you don't have time to have that chat now, or maybe that person is not available.

2. There are two ways to fill in the Next Action field.

3. If you are in the folder view looking at multiple messages.

Click on the message and then click the Message Options icon on the Quick Access toolbar to open the message properties window, see Chapter 11 to setup Quick Access Toolbar. The figure below shows the Message Options icon installed on the Quick Access toolbar.

4. If you have the message opened in full screen, you can click the More options box on the Tag section of the Ribbon to access the message properties window.

5. Once you have the message properties window open, you can fill in your Next Action in the contacts field (remember we renamed this in your message views to Next Action). As an example you could enter "@Agenda Joe – Check on the latest status of the E2 Project".

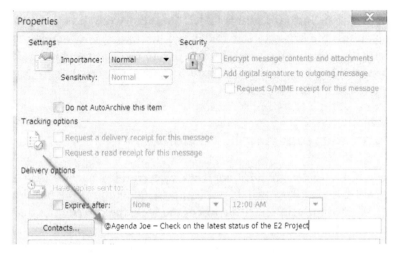

6. This note will now appear in your CYD folder views under Next Action, since you added @Agenda to the front, it will also appear in your @Agenda context folder.

@Calls

1. You would follow the same steps above but instead of @Agenda, you will enter @Call as the starting text in Contacts field.

2. Your @Calls folder looks for all messages that have an active follow-up flag and the text "@Call" in the contacts field which will then display the message you just updated.

@Someday-Maybe

This context folder is a bit different from the others. The criteria for this folder only looks for messages that have the @Someday-Maybe category selected. Messages do not have to have an active follow-up flag to be included in this folder. This allows you to push future plans and projects into this folder and not have them come up as reminders in your daily system. You should look as part of a weekly or monthly review so you can refresh your mind from time to time about these wish list projects

Working from your !CYD Folder

The !CYD folder provides one view of everything in your system that is overdue, on schedule or planned for the future. The overdue messages appear in red at the top of the view, the current messages appear in the middle of the view and the planned messages appear further down the view. This is a giant shift from the way Outlook organizes messages in the normal inbox with older messages just getting pushed further and further down into the folder view. The messages that you assigned Next Actions to also appear in !CYD since they have a follow-up flag. This is a great feature, if you neglect your context lists, you will still see those messages in your !CYD folder.

Since this folder includes messages from your inbox and your sent folder, you have one complete view to your complete workload. As you are working this folder, it is very easy to change the sort to view by sender, receiver, subject or date.

When you are in this folder, you goal should be to clear out items that are in red. These items are overdue and require some action on your part. Before you clear out an item from this view, you should highlight that message and then click the subject header at the top of the view to sort by subject. You can then see if there are other messages in the thread and delete or file those messages at the same time, this will go a long way towards keeping a clean inbox and not chasing others for work they have already responded to.

Divert the Noise

CYD will be much easier to implement if you route informational, non-action type messages around the system. I am sure you receive emails today that you need to have for reference but you don't necessarily have to read when they arrive. This could be messages addressed to a distribution list, received from a mailing list or other schedule mailing services. There are a couple of ways to accomplish this. You can setup a rule to move the messages as they arrive to a folder that your CYD folders do not search. You could add an exception to the CYD rule to exclude these messages. Or you could add a separate rule that fires before the CYD rule that moves those messages and then Stops Rules Processing, this way the message will not be flagged by the CYD rule.

10

WEEKLY REVIEW

Chapter Plan

◊   Implement a weekly review process

A weekly review(another David Allen GTD concept) is an opportunity to step outside of the day to day and make sure you are on track and focused on the right projects and tasks. CYD provides tools to manage, categorize and prioritize your work flow through the use of the CYD, Context and Project folders discussed in earlier chapters. The goal of the weekly review is to clean out and re-prioritize the content in your folders (lists).

You should try to define a scheduled time each week to perform your weekly review. I try to block out time on Fridays to accomplish this, if my schedule gets too hectic, I sometimes switch to bi-weekly or even monthly reviews at times. This is not optimum, my point is that everything I've talked about in this book is flexible. You can't let your system control you, it is there to support you. I have listed out the key components of a successful weekly review and the detailed steps on how to complete the review.

Here are the key components of the CYD Weekly Review

◊ Clean out overdue messages from your CYD folder (clear out everything in red - Overdue).

◊ Review your Someday-Maybe folder and determine if anything should be set to active status.

◊ Review your project folders and remove any folders that are no longer relevant.

◊ Review your category list and remove any categories that are no longer relevant.

◊ Move your completed messages from Inbox to InboxPro (ignore if you have the auto-filing macro setup).

Clean out overdue messages from the CYD folder

This can be the most challenging part of the weekly review. Your goal should be to review every message in red and take some type of action to move that message forward, use the 4D's,(Do It, Delegate it Defer it, Delete it). If you've done a good job during the week staying on top of your messages, you should be able to get through this. I have to be honest again, I do a fair amount of traveling and when I am on the road, it is difficult to stay on top of my email. Occasionally I end up with messages that are a couple of weeks old. I really don't like this feeling, because those messages could be related to commitments I have made to others.

The most recent addition to CYD - the Due Today folder - has really helped me to stay on top of email. When traveling or tied up in meetings, I try to block out time each day to get through the Due Today folder. I may not be able to get to my overdue messages from the CYD folder, but at least I can look at what has come due today and try to deal with that. This way at least those messages won't add to the backlog. This has really helped me to stay on top of my email. I used to go into my weekly reviews with a hundred or more emails outstanding, since I have been using the Due Today folder, that number has been drastically reduced.

Review your Someday-Maybe Folder

I love my Someday-Maybe folder. It is a place for me to send messages that are not urgent or important but that I don't want to lose touch with. I send messages over to Someday-Maybe by assigning the @ Someday-Maybe category and then clearing the follow-up flag. These messages don't appear in the main CYD folders, so they don't clog up my system. During my weekly review, I always take a few minutes to look through this folder to see if there is anything that I want to bring back to an active state. I just flag the message for follow-up and then enter a Next Action so I can get the particular project or task back into my active queue.

Review your Projects Folders

As I mentioned in earlier chapters, the project folders can be used to create temporary workspaces to collect messages about a common subject. You can set any criteria you want for a project folder like category, sender, subject, etc... Take a look through your project folders and see if any of them can be removed. The messages will still be saved in your physical folders, all you are doing is deleting the virtual search folder.

Before you remove a project folder, take a look through the messages. If any of them have a follow-up flag set, decide if you want to clear out that follow-up flag or if you still have work to do on that particular message. Review the rest of your project folders to determine if there are any Next Actions you can define to move those projects forward.

Review your Category Lists

You don't have to do this during every weekly review, but it is a good idea to review your category list on a regular basis and remove categories you are no longer using. For example I might have created a category named p.AugTexasTrip to collect messages for that trip in a single project folder. Once that trip is complete, I no longer need that category. When you delete a category from the master list, it does not remove that category from the assigned messages.

Move your Completed Messages

Back in Chapter 5, I demonstrated how to either setup a macro to auto-file your completed messages or manually move them from Inbox to InboxPro. If you are not using the auto-file macro then you can take some time during your weekly review to move your completed messages from your Inbox to your Inbox-Pro. This will keep your Inbox clean and also reduce the number of messages you see on your smart phone, if you have it connected to your email.

Finally, once you finish your weekly review, take a few minutes to pat yourself on the back. I talk to people regularly about how they manage their day and I can tell you, most of them never take the time to clean up their systems, that is if they even have a system. The result for you is less stress, better job performance and a feeling of control. Nice work!

11

OUTLOOK CONFIGURATION RECAP

Chapter Plan

◊ Review the configuration changes needed to support CYD in Microsoft Outlook

Here are the suggested changes to fully support CYD. Some of these changes were covered in previous chapters but not all, so please double check each item below to make sure you have it configured correctly for CYD.

Click **File, Options** and then make the following changes in each section noted.

Mail Section

◊ Message Arrival section: Uncheck all the boxes, you don't need the constant interruptions every time a message arrives.

Calendar Section

◊ Work Time: Uncheck Sunday and Saturday, this way when you push a message forward for follow-up this week or next week, it will come due on Friday instead of Saturday. If you prefer to do your weekly review on Saturday, then you can leave the Saturday box checked.

Advanced Section

Outlook Start and Exit

◊ Click the **Browse** button and select **!Due Today by String** as the folder to start outlook in.

◊ Click the button for Auto Archive Settings.

◊ Uncheck the option to Run AutoArchive every 14 days. AutoArchive is a dangerous feature in Outlook when it comes to CYD. It automatically moves messages to an archive folder that is stored under your user profile in Windows. If this box is checked and you have an IT department, check with them first before you turn it off. You don't need to auto-archive since you will be archiving your messages yourself each year.

Send and Receive

◊   Uncheck the box **Send immediately when connected.**

Customize Ribbon

◊   Check the box next to Developer on the Customize Ribbon window.

Quick Access Toolbar

◊   Select All Commands from the **Choose commands from** dropdown, highlight Message Options and Click the add button to include this on your tool bar.

Trust Center

1. Click **Trust Center Settings** button.

2. Click Macro Settings from the left side bar.

3. Select the radio button for **"Notifications for all macros"**, click **OK**

12

END OF YEAR CLEANUP

Chapter Plan

◊   Clean up your system and get ready for another year

Wow another year has passed. It is time to clean out your CYD system to prepare for the new year. End of year cleanup is definitely made easier thanks to CYD. I will walk you through the process of closing out the files for the current year and also how to manage messages that are going to flow into the new year. I would suggest you perform these steps around the second week of January, that should give you time to clear out most of the messages from the past year. If you have messages that are still active from the past year, you can either forward them to yourself, creating a new message or just leave them in your active files. You can always go back at a later date and move any stragglers over to your archive files at that time.

Clean out messages you don't need to archive

Before you begin the archive process, I suggest you open your InboxPro folder and sort by size and review any messages that are large (say more than 5 mb) and decide if you really need to archive those messages or if you can just delete them. Do the same for your Sent folder. I bet a few of those larger messages contain videos or photos you shared with others that don't really need to be archived and backed up.

1. Open the **InboxPro** folder.

2. Click the **Size column** to sort by size, you should have the largest messages at the top.

3. Review the messages that are larger than 1 or 2 megabytes, highlight the messages you don't need to save, right click and select **Delete**.

4. Complete steps 1 thru 3 for your **Sent** folder.

 Backup your Outlook File before you begin this process. Check with your IT department and let them know what you are doing before you start. They may have requirements in regards to the storage of archived email messages.

Archive your completed messages

I am going to walk you through the process of creating storage folders and then moving those folders to an archive .PST file. Outlook stores its data in a file with a .PST file extension, unless you are on Exchange, then its a .OST file. In either case you can still create a .PST file for archive purposes.

1. Right click on your mailbox name in the Outlook folder tree on the left side of the screen and select **New Folder.**

2. Type In **Archive-20xx** (replace xx with the past year) and click **OK.**

3. Scroll down the folder tree and find the folder you just created.

4. Right click on the Archive folder, select **New Folder** and enter **Inbox-20xx** as the folder name and then click **OK.**

5. Right click again on the Archive folder, select **New Folder** and enter **Sent-20xx** as the Folder name and click **OK.**

In steps 4 and 5 replace the xx with the past year. Your folders should look like the ones listed below. In the example 2012 represents the "past" year.

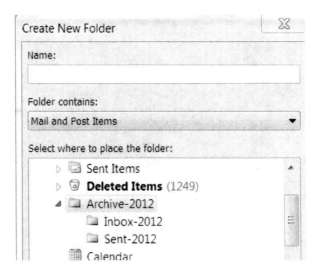

Archive folders created, now you can start to move messages.

1. Click on your **InboxPro** folder.

2. Click the **Flag icon** to sort your messages by follow-up flag status. You want the messages with no flag at the top.

3. Click the first message, then hold the Shift Key down and Highlight all of the messages with an empty follow-up status.

4. Right click on any highlighted message and select **Move** and then select your **Inbox-20xx** folder. Outlook will move the messages to the archive folder. If you have a large amount of messages, you can select a group, move them and go back and repeat the process until they have all been moved.

5. You should be left with only messages that still have an active follow-up flag.

6. Repeat the same process above to move messages from your Sent folder to your Sent-20xx folder.

7. Right click on your **Inbox-20xx** folder and click **Properties** and select the radio button **Show total number of items**. Write down the message count that appears to the right of the folder. This is the number of messages you have in the folder.

8. Repeat step 7 for your Sent-20xx folder.

Your messages are now moved to the archived folders, the last step is to move those folders to a separate archive data file. Again please check with your IT department before you do this if you are a corporate user.

1.   Click **New Items** from the Outlook Ribbon and then click **More items** and select **Outlook Data File**.

2.   Click **OK** to choose Outlook data file (.pst).

3.   Decide where you want to store this file on your hard drive.

4.   I suggest you name the file Outlook Archive 20xx (replace xx with the archive year).

5.   You will be returned to Outlook's main screen, you should now see that archive file listed on the folder tree on the left.

6.   Right click on the **Archive-20xx** folder you created earlier and select **Move Folder** and select the Outlook Archive file you created, click **OK** to move the folders.

Once Outlook completes the move process, click on the Outlook Archive file and open up the folders and make sure your messages are all there. Repeat steps 7 and 8 from above and check your message counts to the ones you wrote down to make sure they match. There is no reason they shouldn't match, but if they don't you will need to open up your backup PST file and try again.

Cleanup Your System

Take a walk through your project folders and your category folders, remove anything that is no longer needed.

Final Close Out

If you were unable to close out all your prior year messages when you did the archive, you may want to go back at a later date and move the last of the messages to the archive. Once you have completed that, you can close the archive file. If you need messages from that file, you can always go back and open it up and reference those messages. To close the file, just right click on it and select Close.

To open the file and reference the messages, just click File and then select Open and Open Outlook Data File. Locate the file on your hard drive and open it.

Please make sure to include this file in your backup process or at least save a copy of it to some alternate media such as a USB drive, DVD or cloud backup service.

EMAIL MANAGEMENT TIPS

Chapter Plan

◊ Share email best practices

Manage informational content you receive

Scheduled reports, newsletters, industry updates, all valuable content, but you don't want this information dragging your system down.

◊ Unsubscribe from mailings that come too often or provide little or no value.

◊ Setup a rule to route these messages to a dedicated folder that you can use for reference. This is the one exception to the CYD rule. Here is an example, I receive status reports each day on our servers and systems. I don't need to view these when they arrive, but if a problem happens I need to access them to monitor the situation. For these messages, I immediately move them to a folder I created called System Alerts. This folder is not included in my CYD search folders criteria so these messages don't gunk up my CYD folders. I did the same for mailing lists that I am subscribed to.

Email Etiquette

◊ Always direct an email message to one person in the body of the message. Avoid addressing it to the attention of a group or more than one person.

◊ If you are responding to a long worded message, bullet out the key points and respond under those bullets.

◊ Be careful with the user of Reply All.

◊ Be cognizant of the addresses listed in the TO and the CC section. Many people filter messages to just focus on ones where their name appears in the To: section.

◊ Try to get your message across in one screen of text; most people don't have time to read more than that. You have a better chance of getting a quick response if you make the message clear and concise.

Email Attachments

◊ Create a folder structure on your computer to store messages by project, customer, etc. Save the attachments to those folders and delete them from the email messages. This will greatly reduce the size of your Outlook storage files.

◊ If you have multiple messages in a thread with attachments and it is an active thread, move the attachments to the latest message, you can delete the earlier messages in the thread. You can do this by editing the current message and then pasting the attachment into the message.

◊ Sort your InboxPro and sent folders by size and check through the emails with larger attachments, delete the ones you don't need to save. This is especially important if you send and receive a lot of photos and videos via email.

Touch Each Message One Time

Think about it, how many times to you look at the same message in Outlook? You might look at the message, realize you don't have time to deal with it and then come back and do the same thing 3 or 4 more times before finally doing something. If you decide to defer the message to a later time, make sure to enter a Next Action so that when you do come back to the message, you will know what you need to do next without having to re-read the message. You can take that one step further and define a context like @Work, @Call to group this message for later processing.

Use the "Four Ds for Decision Making" model

Action	Outcome
Do It	2 minutes or less, just do it!
Delegate It	Forward and set follow-up flag
Defer It	Set Next Action and follow-up flag
Delete It	Clear flag to file it or just delete it

APPENDIX – STEP BY STEP INSTRUCTIONS

Control Your Day Checklist

☐ Create a folder named InboxPro under your Inbox.

☐ Create a rule to flag each message you receive for follow-up today.

☐ Create the auto-filing macro (optional advanced feature).

☐ Add Due Date and Contact fields to your default compact view.

☐ Add the Message Options icon to your toolbar.

☐ Create the !CYD Folder include messages from Inbox and Sent that have a follow-up flag.

☐ Create the !Due Today folder (same as !CYD) and then sort by date and show conversations.

☐ Create the !Today folder, (same as !CYD) and add category = !Today.

☐ Create your @Context folders filtering active messages by context.

☐ Remove follow-up flags from existing inbox/sent messages that no longer require action.

☐ Create an archive folder and move all your existing inbox messages to this folder.

CHAPTER 3 MOVING FROM FOLDERS TO CATEGORIES

Add the main CYD Categories to your list

1. Open up your category list through one of the following methods.

2. Right click on a message, select *Categories* and then select *All Categories*.

3. Click the Home tab, click the *Categorize Icon* and then select *All Categories*.

4. The Categories window shows a listing of all of your categories, you can add, rename or delete categories from this view.

5. Click the **New** button and then type in the category name **@call.**

6. Click the **color drop down** and set it to **none** (using color takes up more space and adds noise to your CYD folders).

7. Click **OK** to save the new category name.

8. Complete steps 3 - 5 to add the following category names @NA, @Read, @Web, @Someday-Maybe, !Today.

9. Once you have finished adding categories, click **OK** to close the Category dialog window.

CHAPTER 4 – CONFIGURE OUTLOOK FOR CYD

Add CYD fields to your default view

1. Click the **View** menu option from above the Outlook ribbon, select **Change View**, select **Manage Views** from the options list.

2. Click the **Compact View** name, click **Modify.**

3. Click the **Columns Button**, find and highlight the **Due Date** field from the window on the left and then click the **Add button** to move **Due Date** from the Available Columns to the Show these columns list.

4. Drag the **Due Date** column and place it just above the From column.

5. Highlight the **Contacts** field from the window on the left and then click the **Add button** to move **Contacts** from the Available Columns to the Show these columns list.

6. Drag the **Contacts** column and place it just below **Subject**.

7. Drag the **Categories** column and place it below the **Contacts** column and click **OK**.

8. Click the **Format Columns** button and then click on the **Contact** column in the available fields list. Change the label from **Contacts** to **Next Action**, Click **OK** on all three windows to close out the Manage All Views window.

9. Click the **Change View** option again, and select **Apply current view to other mail folders**.

10. The top folder (your mailbox) should be checked, click **OK** to apply the new view to your mailbox.

11. Any new folder you create from this point forward will have the Due Date, Next Action and Categories columns displayed correctly.

Create your !CYD Folder

1. Right click on the **Search Folder**s link in the folder tree and select **New Search Folder**.

2. Drag the scroll bar to the bottom of the New Search Folder Options and select **Create a custom Search Folder** and then click the **Choose button** at the bottom of the window.

3. Enter **!CYD** as the Name of the search folder.

4. Click the **Criteria Button** and then click the **More Choices** Tab, check the box "**Only Items Which: are flagged by me** and then click **OK**.

5. Click the **Browse button**, check the box next to **Inbox** and **Sent Items,** make sure to uncheck the box at the very top, the default is to search all folders. Leave the **include**

Subfolders box checked. Click **OK** and then **OK** again to save your changes.

6. Click the **!CYD** folder to show its contents in the main screen, if you have any messages in the folder, they are messages that are in your sent or inbox that you may have flagged in the past. You can leave them for now, you will clean out these flags before you start using CYD.

Create the !Due Today Folder

1. Right click on the **Search Folders** link in the folder tree on the left side of outlook and select **New Search Folder.**

2. Drag the scroll bar to the bottom of the New Search Folder Options and select **Create a custom Search Folder** and then click the **Choose button** at the bottom of the window.

3. Enter **!Due Today** as the Name of the search folder.

4. Click the **Criteria Button** and then click the **More**

Choices Tab, check the box **Only Items Which: are flagged by me.**

5. Click the **Advanced Tab** in the Search Folder Criteria window and the click the **Field button,** select **All Mail Fields,** click the **Due Date** Field, set the condition = "Today", click the **Add to List button** and finally click **OK.**

6. Click the **Browse button,** check the box next to **Inbox** and **Sent Items,** make sure to uncheck the box at the very top as this defaults to search all folders. Leave the **include Subfolders** box checked. Click **OK** and then OK again to save your changes.

7. Click the **!Due Today** folder, click the **View menu,** click **Date** from the Arrangement Box. Check the box to turn on **Show in Conversations.**

8. Right click on the **Due Date** column header and click **Remove this column,** all messages in this folder are due today.

9. Click the **View tab** in the Ribbon, click **View Settings,** click the **Group By button** and uncheck the box **Automatically Group According to Arrangement.**

 **Sort order must be set to Date, if you change the sort, the conversation thread feature is disabled. To reset, click the View Tab and select Date from the Arrangement Box**

Create the !Today Focus Folder

1. Right click on the **Search Folders** link in the folder tree and select **New Search Folder**.

2. Drag the scroll bar to the bottom of the New Search Folder Options and select **Create a custom Search Folder,** click the **Choose button** at the bottom of the window.

3. Enter **!Today Focus** as the Name of the search folder.

4. Click the **Criteria Button,** click the **More Choices Tab**, check the box **Only Items Which: are flagged by me.**

5. Click the **Categories button** in the same window, Click **New** to add a new category and add the category **!Today,** change the color to green or any other color you like. This is the one category I like to assign a color to so it stands out in all folder views.

6. Find the **!Today category** in your list and check the box next to it, click **OK**.

7. Click the **Advanced Tab** in the Search Folder Criteria window, click the **Field button**, select **All Mail Fields** and then click the **Due Date** Field, set the **condition** = "Today", click the **Add to List button,** click **OK**.

8. Click the **Browse button**, check the box next to **Inbox** and **Sent Items,** make sure to uncheck the box at the very top as this defaults to search all folders. Leave the **include Subfolders** box checked. Click **OK** and then **OK** again to save your changes.

Create the InboxPro Folder

This will be your new storage folder for all received messages that you have marked as completed.

1. Click the **Inbox** from the Outlook folder tree on the left side of the screen.

2. Right click on the Inbox and select **New Folder**.

3. Enter the name as **InboxPro** and make sure **Inbox** is highlighted under **Select where to place folder** so this folder gets created below the Inbox.

Please double check the spelling of the folder name as it has to match exactly for the auto-filing macro to work properly (Chapter 5).

CHAPTER 5 – SETUP CYD RULE AND FILING MACRO

Create the CYD Follow Up Today Rule

1. Click the **Home tab** and then click the **Rules icon** and select **Create Rule**.

2. Click the **Advanced Options button** from the Create Rule window.

3. Click the **Next button** to skip the first window in the Rules Wizard and then click **Yes** to confirm this rule will apply to every message you receive.

4. Check the box **Flag message for follow up at this time**.

5. Click the hyperlink **follow up at this time** in the Step 2 box at the bottom and click **OK** to set **Today** as the for: value.

6. Click the **Next button,** if you want to apply any exceptions you can add them here

7. For example, if you want to exclude messages sent to a distribution list, check the box for **except if sent to people or public group** and then click the link in Step 2 to select the people or group to exclude.

8. Click the **Next button** to move to the final Rules screen.

9. Rename the rule to **CYD Follow Up Today**.

10. Make sure the first check-box **run this rule now** is unchecked and the second check-box **Turn on this rule** is checked. You don't want the rule to run until you clean out your existing Inbox messages.

11. Click the **Finish Button** to save the rule.

Setup rules to auto-assign categories

1. Right click on a message in your inbox, select **Rules** and then **Create Rule**.

2. The first dialog box allows you to set the rule based on the sender, recipient, subject. You can select one of these options or click the **Advanced Options button** to get more options.

3. For this example, check off the From "person's name" box and then click the **Advanced Options button**. You can click the **Next button** to skip the Set Condition dialog box since you already selected the sender name in the step above.

4. Check the box **assign it to a <u>category</u>**, then click the **<u>category</u>** link in the step 2 window at the bottom.

5. Check off the category you want to use or click the **New button** and add a new category and then check it off. You can check off more than one category.

6. Click the **Next Button**, click **Next** again to skip the Exceptions dialog window.

7. You can leave the default name of the rule or change it. If you want the rule to process against all existing messages in your inbox, you can check off that box.

8. Click the **Finish button** to save the rule.

You can repeat this process to build as many auto-categorize rules as you want. You don't have to categorize every message you receive. They will all be stored and accessible through your Inbox and Sent folders, the categories just provide for a better level of grouping.

Filing your Completed Messages

Manual Filing Process

1. Click on your **Inbox**.

2. Click on the **Flag icon** in the column heading section. This will sort your inbox message by follow-up flag status.

3. You should see some messages with an empty flag and others with a red flag. If you don't see the empty flag on any messages, click the **flag icon** again, to reverse the sort.

4. Highlight all of the messages with an empty flag, right click and select **Move** and select the **InboxPro** folder.

5. That's it, you have just filed all of your completed messages, could it BE any easier?

If you would like to automate the filing process, you can follow the steps below. This gets a bit tricky, and you may run into some issues if your IT department has locked down your ability to access admin features within Outlook.

This macro will run automatically once it is setup. DO NOT proceed with these steps until you are ready to implement CYD. This macro will move all completed messages from your Inbox to your InboxPro folder when you exit Outlook.

Create CYD Auto-Filing Macro

1. Your will first need to allow macros to run in Outlook, if you do not have admin access to your machine and Outlook you may need to get assistance from your IT department.

2. Click the **File Tab**, then select **Options**, then **Trust Center**.

3. Click the **Trust Center Options button.**

4. Click **Macro Settings** and then select the radio button option **Notifications for all Macros** .

5. This will allow the macro to run when you start outlook but will first give you a warning and ask you to confirm before starting Outlook each time.

6. Click **OK** on each window to close the options window.

7. Turn on the Developer Tab.

   ◊ Click the **File tab**, then select **Options, Customize Ribbon.**

   ◊ On the right side of the screen you will see the main tabs, check the box next to the **Developer Tab**, then click **OK** to close the Options window.

8. Click the **Developer Tab** and then click the **Visual Basic icon.**

9. From the folder view on the left side, click the **Project1 folder**, then the **Microsoft Outlook Objects folder** and finally double click on **ThisOutlookSession** to open up the code window.

10. Paste the following code into the open window.

```
Private Sub Application_Quit()
FileCompletedInboxMessages
End Sub
Sub FileCompletedInboxMessages()
Dim myOlApp As New Outlook.Application
Dim myNameSpace As Outlook.NameSpace
Dim myInbox As Outlook.MAPIFolder
Dim myDestFolder As Outlook.MAPIFolder
Dim myItems As Outlook.Items
Dim myItem As Object
Set myNameSpace = myOlApp.GetNamespace("MAPI")
Set myInbox = myNameSpace.
GetDefaultFolder(olFolderInbox)
Set myItems = myInbox.Items
Set myDestFolder = myInbox.Folders("InboxPro")
' User cleared the follow-up flag
Set myItem = myItems.Find("[FLAGSTATUS] = 0")
While TypeName(myItem) <> "Nothing"
myItem.Move myDestFolder
Set myItem = myItems.FindNext
Wend

' User marked as completed
Set myItem = myItems.Find("[FLAGSTATUS] = 1")
While TypeName(myItem) <> "Nothing"
myItem.Move myDestFolder
Set myItem = myItems.FindNext
Wend
End Sub
```

11. Click **File** and then click **Close and Return to Microsoft Outlook.**

12. Shut down Microsoft Outlook, click **Yes** to close the dialog box and save the VBA project.

13. Open Outlook you should see the security notice dialog window. Click the **Enable Macros button** to start outlook.

14. Your CYD Filer is now setup, each time you close outlook. The macro will fire and move all messages that have been completed from your Inbox to your InboxPro folder.

Create Your Next Actions Search Folder

This search folder will include all active messages from your Inbox and Sent Items folder with any value in the Contacts(Next Action) field.

Search Folder	Purpose
@Agenda	Topics to be discussed with others
@Calls	Telephone calls you need to make
@NA	Any message with a Next Action
@Web	Action requires access to the web
@Read	Articles/content you need to read
@WF	Messages waiting for a response
@Someday-Maybe	A folder to store wish list items

1. Right click on **Search Folders** in the Outlook folder tree on the left side of the screen and click **New Search Folder.**

2. Scroll to the bottom of the screen and double click **Create a custom Search Folder** under the Custom option.

3. Enter the folder name, for example **@NA** *Include only active messages*

4. Click the **Criteria button**, click on the **More Choices Tab.**

5. Check off **Only items which: are flagged by me.** *Include all messages that have a value in the Contacts field (Next Action)*

6. Click the **Advanced Tab**, click the **Field** button to open the fields dropdown.

7. Select **All Mail fields** and then select **Contacts** and set the condition to **is not empty,** click the button **add to List**, click the **OK** Button.

8. Click the **Add to List** button

9. Click the **OK** button to return to the Custom Search Folder window.

10. Click the **Browse** button to select the physical folders to include, un-check your mailbox and then check the **Inbox** and **Sent Items**. Make sure to leave the **Search subfolders** box checked.

11. Click the **OK** button to close the Select Folders window, Click **OK** to close the Custom search folder window.

Create Specific Context Folders

Follow the steps below to create each Context folder

1. Right click on **Search Folders** in the Outlook folder tree on the left side of the screen and click **New Search Folder.**

2. Scroll to the bottom of the screen and double click **Create a custom Search Folder** under the Custom option.

3. Enter the folder name, **@Agenda** *Include only active messages*

4. Click the **Criteria button,** click on the **More Choices Tab.**

5. Check off **Only items which: are flagged by me.** *Include messages that match the criteria for the search folder*

6. Click the **Advanced Tab,** click the **Field** button to open the fields dropdown.

7. Select **All Mail fields** and then select **Contacts** and leave the condition as **contains** and then type **@Agenda** in the **Value** box.

8. Click the **Add to List** button.

9. Click the **OK** button to return to the Custom Search Folder window.

10. Click the **Browse** button to select the physical folders to include, un-check your mailbox and then check the **Inbox** and **Sent Items**. Make sure to leave the **Search subfolders** box checked.

11. Click the **OK** button to close the Select Folders window, Click **OK** to close the Custom search folder window.

Repeat the steps above for each @Context folder, you can build all of the search folders listed above or just select the contexts you want to focus on. Change the folder name in Step 3 and the criteria in Step 7 to match the context folder you are creating.

Follow the same steps to create the Someday-Maybe folder, skip steps 4 and 5. This will allow you to clear the follow-up flag on Someday-Maybe messages. They will appear in the Someday-

Maybe context folder but they will not appear in your CYD, Due Today or !Today's Focus folders. If you want to remove an item from your Someday-Maybe folder, you can either delete it or remove the Someday-Maybe category assignment.

Advanced Section

Microsoft Outlook provides an advanced query builder but it is disabled by default. To enable this feature, you will need to make a change to your Windows Registry. If you are not familiar with editing the Registry please skip this section and work with the context folders as they are described above.

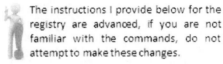

The instructions I provide below for the registry are advanced, if you are not familiar with the commands, do not attempt to make these changes.

Turn on Query Builder in Microsoft Windows

1. Close Outlook.

2. Start the Windows Registry editor.

3. Locate the registry subkey: (14.0 = Office 2010) HKEY_ CURRENT_USER\Software\Microsoft\Office\14.0\ Outlook.

4. Right click on Outlook and choose New Key and enter QueryBuilder.

5. Close the registry editor and restart Outlook.

Expand the critera for your @Calls Context Search Folder

1. Right click on your **@Calls** Search Folder and choose **customize this search folder**.

2. Click the **Criteria** button, you should now see a Query Builder Tab.

3. Click the Advanced Tab and Remove the existing criteria, **Contacts contains @Call.**

4. Click the **Query Builder tab**.

5. Click **Field** button, select **All Mail Fields**, Select **Contacts**, criteria **Contains @Call**, Click **Add to List** Button.

6. Repeat step 5 for the Subject field, same criteria.

7. Change the **Logical Group** to **OR**, Click OK and OK again to save the folder changes.

8. The @Calls folder will now show any active messages that have @Call in the Subject or the Contact field.

Create a Project Folder

1. Right click on **Search Folders** in the Outlook folder tree on the left side of the screen and click **New Search Folder.**

2. Scroll to the bottom of the screen and double click **Create a custom Search Folder** under the Custom option.

3. Enter the folder name, for example **p.2013 Budget Plans**.

4. Click the **Criteria button**, click on the **More Choices Tab**.

5. If you want to include messages with a follow-up flag, check off **Only items which: are flagged by me**, if you want to include all messages from your Inbox, InboxPro and Sent folders, leave this box unchecked.

6. Set any additional criteria for this folder. In most cases you will probably click the categories button and create a new category to assign to messages that will be included in this folder. You can you any of the folder criteria options available.

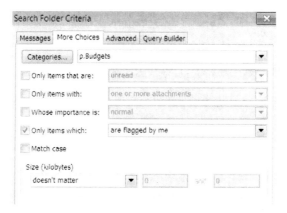

7. Your screen should look similar to the figure above. Click **OK** to close out the criteria screen.

8. Click the **Browse button** to set the physical folder to include in the search.

9. Remove the check next to your mailbox and check off the **Inbox** and the **Sent Items** folder. Make sure the **Search Subfolders box** is checked at the bottom of the screen.

10. Click **OK** on each of the screens to save your new project folder

Clean out your existing Inbox

1. Create Inbox-Old

   ◊ Right click on your **inbox** and select **New Folder.**

   ◊ Enter **Inbox-Old** as the name and make sure **Inbox** is highlighted to create the new folder under your **Inbox** folder.

2. Click on your **Inbox** to show all your messages.

3. Select all the messages, you can click on the first message once, then click the scroll bar to the right and drag the window down to the last message. Hold down the **Shift key** and click your mouse on the last message to highlight them all.

4. Right click on a selected message and then select **Move** and pick **Inbox-Old** from the dropdown list. When you select the folder, Outlook will start moving your messages.

 This next step could take some time if you have a larger number of email messages stored in your Inbox

5. Once Outlook finishes, you will have a completely empty Inbox.

6. If any of the messages from your Inbox had a follow-up flag set, they will still appear in your CYD folders. If you

don't want them to show up, you need to clear the follow-up flag on all messages stored in your Inbox-Old folder. You can follow the steps listed below for the Sent folder.

Your Inbox is EMPTY, take a moment and enjoy this feeling it doesn't happen very often.

Remove Follow-up Flags from any Sent messages

1. Click on your **Sent folder.**

2. Highlight all messages in your Sent folder (see steps above).

3. Right click on a highlighted message, click **Follow-up** and then select **Clear Flag**.

4. This will remove any follow-up flags you may have set in the past out outbound messages. You could leave these follow-up flags in place if you want the messages included in your CYD folders.

CHAPTER 11 – OUTLOOK CONFIGURATION REVIEW

Here are the suggested changes to fully support CYD. Some of these changes were covered in previous chapters but not all, so please double check each item below to make sure you have it configured correctly for CYD.

Click **File, Options** and then make the following changes in each section noted.

Mail Section

Message Arrival section: Uncheck all the boxes; you don't need the constant interruptions every time a message arrives.

Calendar Section

Work Time: Uncheck Sunday and Saturday, this way when you push a message forward for follow-up this week or next week, it will come due on Friday instead of Saturday. If you prefer to do your weekly review on Saturday, then you can leave the Saturday box checked.

Advanced

Outlook Start and Exit

1. Click the Browse button and select !Due Today by String as the folder to start outlook in.

2. Click the button for Auto Archive Settings.

    a. Uncheck the option to Run AutoArchive every 14 days. AutoArchive is a dangerous feature in Outlook when it comes to CYD. It automatically moves messages to an archive folder that is stored under your user profile in Windows. If this box is checked and you have an IT department, check with them first before you turn it off. You don't need to auto-archive since you will be archiving your messages yourself each year.

Send and Receive

Uncheck the box Send immediately when connected.

Customize Ribbon

Check the box next to Developer on the Customize Ribbon window.

Quick Access Toolbar

Select All Commands from the Choose commands from dropdown, highlight Message Options and Click the add button to include this on your tool bar.

Trust Center

1. Click Trust Center Settings button.

2. Click Macro Settings from the left side bar.

3. Select the radio button for "Notifications for all macros", click OK

ABOUT THE AUTHOR

Control Your Day is the final result of a work system I have been using and enhancing for the past 5 years. It has allowed me to stay on top of my workload and reduce the time and stress involved in dealing with the daily onslaught of email messages. I hear so many people complaining about how much time they spend trying to stay on top of their email, I truly believe this book can help.

I grew up in New Jersey and now live and work in Richmond, Virginia with my lovely wife, two boys and 1 chocolate Lab.

There is a companion site for the book at www.controlyourday. net and videos on YouTube (search for Jim McCullen). I want you to succeed with CYD, if you have any questions, post them on the CYD forum or contact me through the CYD website.

CPSIA information can be obtained at www.ICGtesting.com
Printed in the USA
LVOW10s0032100115

422262LV00019B/689/P